Scapes

Michael Baldwin

EAKIN PRESS ⚑ Fort Worth, Texas
www.EakinPress.com

The paintings used on section pages have been converted to grey tones for use in this book. They are beautiful in grey, but are astounding in their original colors. The artist is Johnny Bowen.

Upland Jewels on page vii
Steel Creek Sonata, pages 18-19
The Why of White, page 36-37
Eternal Lights, pages 60-61

Copyright © 2012
By Michael Baldwin
Published By NorTex Press
An Imprint of Wild Horse Media Group
P.O. Box 331779
Fort Worth, Texas 76163
1-817-344-7036
www.WildHorseMediaGroup.com
1 2 3 4 5 6 7 8 9
ISBN-10: 1-935632-28-0
ISBN-13: 978-1-935632-28-3
Library of Congress Control Number 2012936014

For Helen, who always provides good ears and good eats.

Acknowledgments

The author gratefully acknowledges the following journals for the publication of the following poems in this book (some in slightly different form):

Beyond The Gate: Commemorating the Centennial of the Fort Worth Poetry Society, April, 2010—Moon of Popping Trees

Commonweal, April 6, 2001—The Heart Has Its Reasons

Ilya's Honey—Fall, 2003—Medusa
Spring, 2004—Blackberry Eden

Louisiana Literature, Spring, 1999—A Threnody in Winter

New Texas, 2002—Lizard Lecture

Touchstone, Winter, 1997—Tupelo Autumn
—Encounter

What Child Is This? Anthology of Poems Against Child Abuse, 2002—What He Died Of

Contents

Landscapes

Chisos Splendor 3
Gonna Be a Hot One. 4
Horse Country. 5
Wildflower Witness 6
Dawn Dancer. 7
Encounter 8
Tupelo Autumn. 9
Song for Sam's Throne 10
Buffalo River Nocturne 11
Mysterium Tremendum. 12
Stillness at War Eagle Crossing. 13
On Golden Pond 14
Hiking Near Ruidoso 15
Moon of Popping Trees 16
Staring Up the Stars 17

Heartscapes

Eclipsed. 21
Medusa. 23
In Absentia. 24
Blackberry Eden 25
Why Is the Speed of Light So Slow? 27
Multiverse 29
TimemiT. 30
Red Rover. 32
Ill Wind. 34
Heart Stone. 35

Mindscapes

Memento Vivre (Remember You Must Live) 39
Waiting 41
When Neither Truth Nor Beauty Come 42
Suicide Sans Sui 43
Ghost Guessed... 45
Angels.. 46
God's Suicide Note 47
Pictures 48
Global Warming 49
Lizard Lecture 51
Not About Butterflies................................... 52
Wasps 53
Meditation on Basho's Frog............................. 54
Metamorphosis 55
Journey 56
Moondrunk Lunar Eclipse.............................. 57
The Why of White...................................... 58
The Heart Has Its Reasons............................. 59

Soulscapes

Abortion 63
What He Died Of 64
Hunger for Genius 65
Personal Permutations 66
Xmas Epiphany... 67
Grocery Epiphany...................................... 68
Loudenitch Plays Adés' *Darkness Visible* 70
El Niño.. 71
Great Blue.. 72
Watching Water Lilies In Rain 74
Flying on Love... 75
Insoulation 76
Threnody in Winter 77

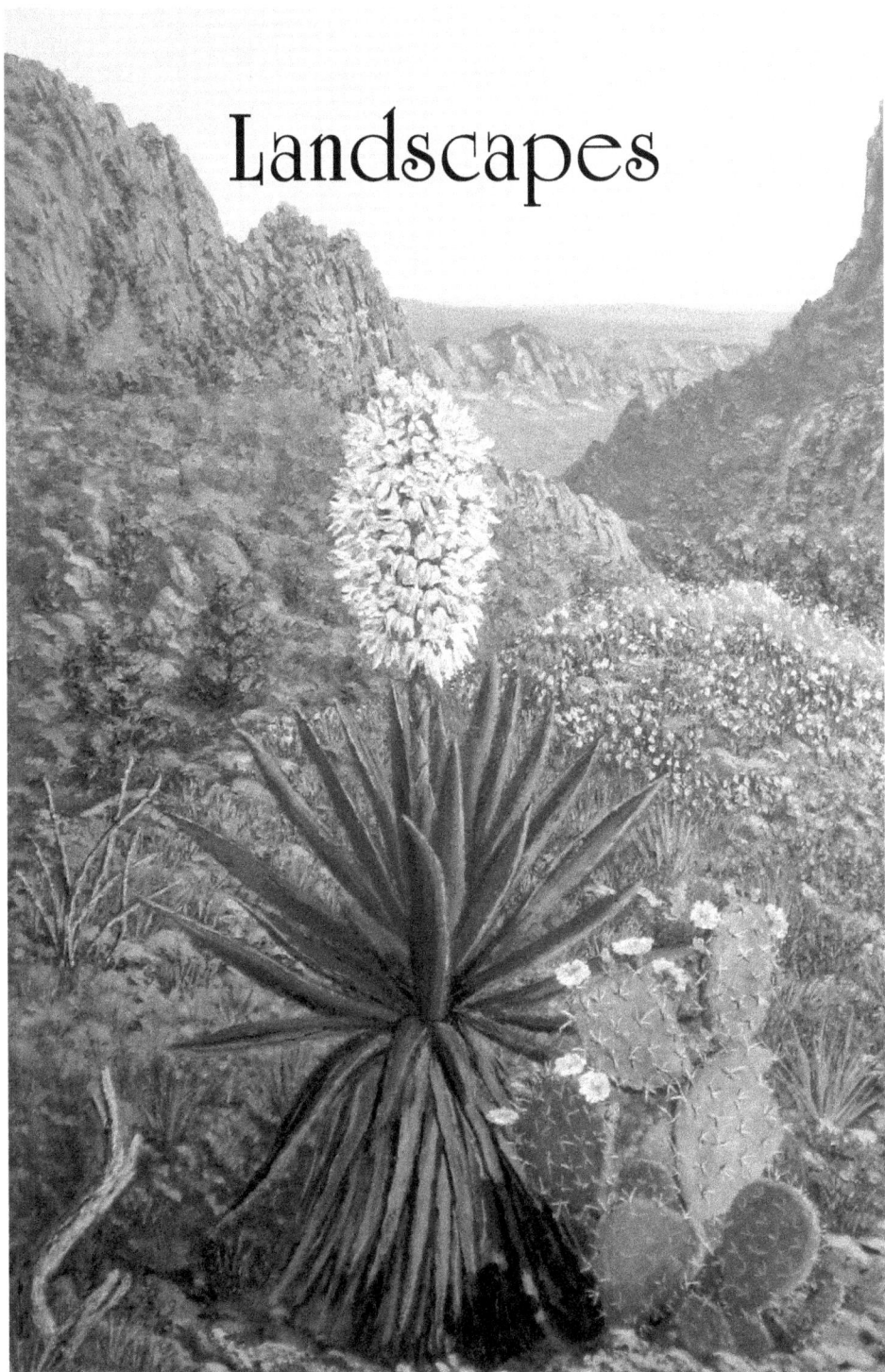

Landscapes

Chisos Splendor

Based on the painting, Chisos Splendor, by Johnny Bowen

We call them Adam's needle,
Giant Dagger, Spanish Bayonet,
and simply Yucca (its Indian name).
The species inhabiting Texas' Chisos
Mountains are particularly
formidable in this country so
arid and sun-battered.

Among these far mountains
and mesas, boulders and buttes,
Yucca give a thrusting brutal beauty
to a vista of thirsty distance.
In this ecology of bleak fecundity,
Yucca, Big Bend Blue Bonnets,
Desert Marigolds, and Purple Sage
compete not for sunlight, but for water.
So Yucca send tap roots down
hundreds of feet for moisture,
then guard it with sharpness.

In summer, thousands of white flower
bells attract thousands of white moths
that couple the Yucca and bed their eggs
in balls of golden pollen to hatch within
the Yucca's seed pods; a marriage of
mutual necessity between insect and plant.
A mystery and a wonder.

If we could view this scene with God's eye,
we would see the energy of light
becoming the energy of life
in a vast complexity of harmony in diversity,
of extravagance in extremity,
of grace in grim circumstance.
Art is God's eye,
dauntless as Yucca's dagger.

Gonna Be A Hot One

Based on the painting, Gonna Be A Hot One, by Johnny Bowen

Many a Texas ranch has a dilapidated
barn with a corrugated iron roof that,
even though the day's barely begun,
already shimmers with heat waves
and groans complaintively as the rust
hots up, waking the red wasps nesting
in its rafters to buzz out and patrol their
harsh domain of Goat-Head, Bull-Nettle,
Purple Thistle, and grotesque green Osage
Oranges (uneaten since the giant ground
sloth went extinct twenty millennia ago),
freshly fallen from the Bois D'arcs along
the fence line, vainly oozing thick sticky
syrup in the sun, where only Prickly Pear
actually revel in the heat, blooming
extravagantly for desultory bees.
Yes, it's gonna be a hot one!

Horse Country

Based on the painting, Texas Tranquility, by Johnny Bowen

These bouldered buttes that signature
the north central Texas plains,
were not thrust up from surrounding scape,
but were left standing by the subsidence
of an ancient shallow sea some hundred
million years ago, when dinosaurs dominated.
Fossils of marine creatures: trilobites,
ammonites, mussels, and spiral snails,
like hard white ghosts, now haunt these
desiccated hills, still listening for the sea.

This is mostly cattle country now, but some
300 years ago, it was prairie grass,
trampled to wild flowers by buffalo herds
from here to the far Dakotas, harrowed
and hallowed by horsed Comanche,
Kiowa, Cheyenne, Pawnee, and Sioux.
Ancestors of now placid horses were looted
from Spanish legions to become mounts
for Indians, vaqueros, cowboys, and soldiers,
or escaped to be free roaming mustangs.

For some 200 halcyon years horses made
the Indian nomads of mid-America mystic
warriors of the plains, the greatest horsemen
the world has known, and made possible
the adventuring that conquered the continent.
Now the prairie has become fenced pastures,
furrowed fields, and cedar breaks, but the hills
and the horses remain, perhaps dimly
remembering in boulders and bones
those wilder, wondrous times.

Wildflower Witness

Based on the painting, Spring Tonic, by Johnny Bowen

A mild, wet winter caressed
the earth and spilled
the Texas hills with flowers.
Firewheels whirl,
set blazing crazily
by sun shafts reclaiming
fresh-washed prairie
from a wandering thunderhead.
Coneflowers,
in ardent yellow,
mock Coronado's El Dorado.
Prickly Pear
save their blooms for summer,
but Bluebonnets
in proud profusion,
like a convocation
of Daughters of the Texas Revolution,
gather reverently around the ruin,
a granite pioneer hearth
forgotten by all but
a pair of hoary oaks,
and spend themselves in beauty
for this itinerant witness.

Dawn Dancer

From the jutting ridgepole
      at the apex of the roof,
like a tiny muezzin in
      a minaret in Mecca,
comes a florid ululation
      like a glory hallelujah,
from the mischief-eyed quick dancer,
      the curved-beaked canyon wren,
announcing the mounting of the morning;
      the light has come again!

I take my coffee on the treetop deck
      on a worn old wicker chair,
warm my hands around the cup,
      and drink, instead, the morning air.
Pale vapors from the sleeping lake,
      its dream-spawned incubi,
perform a sinuous ballet,
      dissolve into the sky.
The still dark hills breathe up the sun
      as a bubble slowly blown,
and nothing other dares to breathe
      till it slips those lips of stone.
The wren, then, jittering on the roof,
      repeats his arioso plea,
and something of my deepest self is,
      for a moment, radiant and free.

Encounter

A fallen Sycamore in cerements of moss

across our path insisted that we sit,

watch the day moon mount

the inner sphere, traversed, too,

by the languorous spiral

of a Red-Tailed Hawk.

Tranced eyes released,

we found ourselves observed:

ten feet away a White-Tail doe

(so still my mind ignored

at first my eye),

now, curiosity complete, snuffed

and deliquesced among the trees.

Where are such easy certainties

of these feral things in us?

Tupelo Autumn

A leathery tupelo leaf,

red with regnant autumn,

still supple,

yet debarked,

finds in its brief falling:

the coriolis urge of air,

the gravitic suck

of sun and planet,

the wave ride

of that spiral tide

of stars that propels it

and us some thousand miles

till earth and leaf

reach each

near the greedy green

spike of a spider lily,

late piercing

deeply acreted

pine straw,

the quiddity

of its little life

unquestioned.

Song for Sam's Throne

Based on the painting, Sam's Throne, by Johnny Bowen

In the misty mountains of Arkansas,
sudden steep deepnesses
at the edge of the highway
can be both heart tightening
and soul exalting.
Motoring thru Newton County,
we parked on a high stone ridge
to view Sam's Throne,
thrust up across the valley
like a defiant green fist.
And having read how Sam Davis,
in the 1820's, anguished at the loss
of his sister, kidnapped by Indians,
ascended that summit each day
for years to shout an angry
garbled gospel that mightily
annoyed his neighbors,
I backed my van to the verge
of that vastness, opened the doors,
with their built-in speakers,
intending to give the valley a hearing
of Vivaldi's gorgeous Gloria,
like a thousand love-crazed angels
rending the universe asunder with song.
But then I noticed the lone hiker resting
on his staff, admiring the sunset,
treasuring the tranquility of this place.
So I just leaned against the van and stared
across at Sam's Throne, illumined
by the golden glance of sunset.
Perhaps that was the hidden gold Sam
bragged about but no one ever found.
A red-shouldered hawk in a nearby tree
silently agreed, and we shared for a moment
the serene magnificence of the mountain.

Buffalo River Nocturne

Based on the painting, Moonlit Serenity, by Johnny Bowen

Nature makes music by night.
Darkness engages our ears
and our imagination with
melodious murmurs,
symphonic susurrations of
water ripples rivering
among rocks, tree tongues
set singing by night breezes,
insects, frogs, and night birds
blending in concert.

But always it is the moon
that enchants the night,
gliding among glowing clouds,
casting such etheric luminance
upon the water that all beings
become imaginary,
become ghosts of themselves,
even our selves.

So, wading elk may be spirits
from an age before man,
manifesting when moonlight,
bent back into its own albedo
by moon's and water's mirrors,
becomes a sacred, timeless,
noctilucent, entranced
entrance for imaginings.

Thus the night mind
mothers our ancient children
and sings them lullaby.

Mysterium Tremendum*

Based on the painting, Hawksbill Crag, by Johnny Bowen

The huge outcropping of ancient,
eroded limestone known as Hawksbill Crag
leaps from the wooded mountainside
into the void above the valley
and cries out in awe and wonder
as it hangs over that vastness,
still grasping the mountain with
inward claws, while gasping
in astonishment, not at the beauty
of the vista, but with startled terror
and exhilaration in the immense
space of this million-year moment.
Does the sow bear sense
the vertiginous spirit of the scarp
as she guards her cubs upon the crag?
Can only the human mind
experience this exalting fall
toward the infinite, this soul-shock
of the sublime?

---

*Mysterium Tremendum (fearful mystery). The spiritual terror provoked by an overpower-
ing spiritual experience.

Stillness at War Eagle Crossing

Based on the painting, War Eagle Crossing, by Johnny Bowen

There is something in nature
that needs essential stillness.
Yes, water loves movement,
loves to shimmer sunlight
in your eyes as it shivers
down a streamway.
Air, too, is enamored with
pushing clouds about the sky
and setting trees atremble.
But nature finds some deep
satisfaction in the utter stillness
of a moment's eon,
as when a Great Blue Heron,
poising for a strike,
exactly imitates the arch
of this abandoned bridge.
So both become integral
as nature meditates in
perfect stillness;
as the universe itself
pauses   for an OM instant
between inhale
and exhale,
to contemplate
this perfect beauty.

On Golden Pond

Based on the painting, Gillett Farms Mallards, by Johnny Bowen

How could a swamp, created by
flooding a lowland stand of timber,
drowning the trees in the process,
to create a killing pond for ducks,
be deemed beautiful?
Yet, when the air is overcast
with a turbid damp that oozes
into your bones, and, with that moist
density, refracts the dawning sunlight
into a diffuse, lambent, golden nimbus,
even the stark trees, stripped skeletal
by an ice storm, shivering naked
on the chill, glowing pond mirror,
instill an eldritch beauty that beckons
the ducks to descend, hens first,
then the emerald-headed drakes,
their braking feathers whistling,
until, just before touching water,
they sense the terrible
stillness of the decoys.

Hiking Near Ruidoso

for Gary, Julia, and Rosemary

Guided by the twisting stream, we ascend
the Sierra Blanca, where Blue Spruce,
Quaking Aspen, and Ponderosa Pine
(its bark the aroma of butterscotch),
block all but a few sharp slants
of sun that scatter glitterings
from tumbling water
and probe the gaps of fallen giants.

Mere yards away from the murmuring rill,
the forest is silent. Birds and insects
move mutely, as if on some secret,
sacred mission.
The earth is adazzle with flowers:
Mexican Thistle, Yellow Salsify,
Fireweed, Scarlet Globe Mallow,
Purple Owl's Clover, Goldenrod.

Orange mushrooms, too, arise beside
boulders clothed in parti-colored lichens,
and fallen trees listen to the silence
with glistening ears of frilly fungi,
listen perhaps for the absent tick
of timefulness,
for the forest has no name for time,
the mountain has no need for time,
nature has no time for time.

The Moon of Popping Trees*

In the moon of popping trees,
when ice glazed branches break
like gun shots or shake glistering
shards upon the bare night prairie,
when the wind voices beckon,
I wrap my bones in a buffalo robe
and crunch across the ground frost,
my feathers pointing the way
to bear hump hill, the vision place,
where I may step out of myself,
to become an antlered shaman
of ancient times, to see
green boughs blossom and fill with fruit,
horse-high prairie grass wimple
with sweet-smelling winds,
and bison, elk, and antelope mingle
in numberless herds, invoking
our worship, providing our plenty.
But these are now just restless ghosts,
almost invisible in the belly of night,
upon this trackless white,
and now there is really nothing here
but the bone white moon,
the mute white snow,
the cold white wind of time.

---

*The Moon of Popping Trees is the lunar month of December for the Lakota

Staring Up The Stars

Based on the painting, Eternal Lights, by Johnny Bowen

Crisp winter nights among mountains

are best for watching the stars.

Only an empty, snow-blown cemetery

can make their viewing even better.

Lean against a century-old gravestone

and let the cold seek your bones

as your eye finds the Northern Cross

bright above the western hills.

Let your mind fall into the stars.

Allow your awareness to wander

the hypnotic vastness of the universe.

If your mind can match the rhythms

of the stars, you may learn to share

their cosmic thoughts.

Stars died to become human.

Native Americans believe we die

to become stars.

Mountains and trees have always

contemplated the stars.

It is the beginning of wisdom.

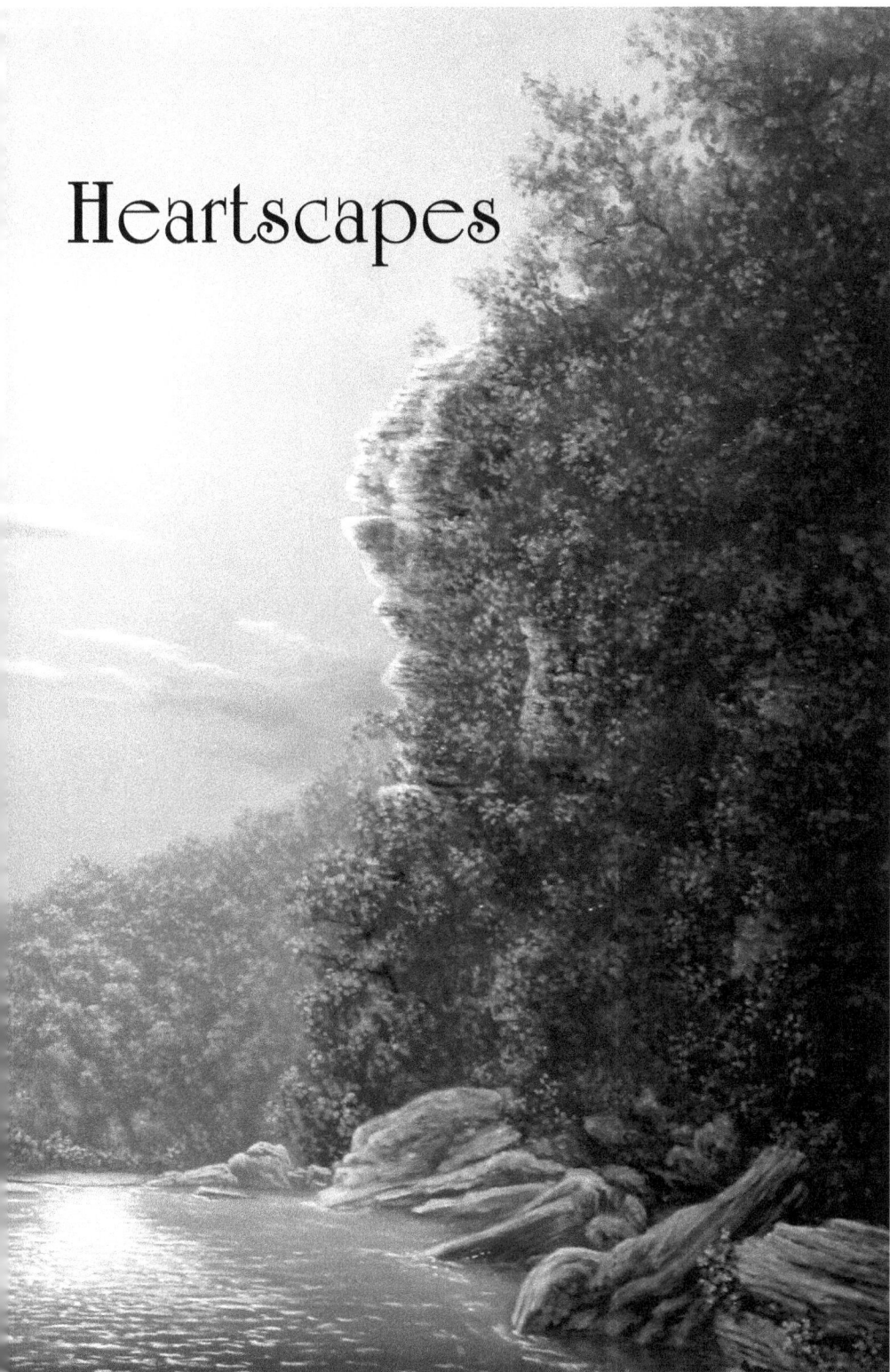

Heartscapes

Eclipsed

For Frank, whose eclipse this was

An eclipse of the human heart is more dramatic than those
      astronomical, if less visible to the casual observer.
The radio said this solar eclipse
      would be the last of the century.
It could be safely viewed by pinhole projection
      onto a simple cardboard screen.
I rigged the apparatus, then left it home and walked
      to Econ 101 across dew damp campus grass.
Forgot the time, of course, and remembered only
      when the sky dimmed and others pointed sunward.
I ran toward home but stopped for traffic at the corner.
      And there, beneath a swaying sycamore,
a girl with a river of cinnabar hair, a Rossetti virgin,
      raised her arms, as if in benediction, and laughed.
Transfixing me with celadon eyes, she exclaimed,
      in innocent delight, "I am eclipsed!"
Coming near I saw her white blouse shimmer
      with dark scimitars, each slicing brightness.
Seeking the cause of this phenomenon, I observed
      the sycamore leaves riddled with insect holes,
each projecting an image of the eclipse,
      so myriad replicas crawled on us like inch worms,
moving dizzily and distorting like Dali's melting
      clocks, as leaves luffed on placid air,
occulting orbs contorting on the contours
      of her blouse as if captured
by the enigmatic gravities of her breasts.
      She held out one pale hand to me
and on its palm the coupled moon and sun
      flowed largo along her heart line.
She seemed to offer everything to me and, smiling,
      touched me gently on my cheek,
her eyes, as vast as ocean skies, engulfed me.
      I stared at her, immesmered,

as she flowed and wavered with eclipses
      like some   unreachable   mirage.
Then she turned and walked away
      into that more than moon-darked day,
her flaming hair swinging,
     voice ringing,
        singing like a child.

Medusa

She reaches back
to the limit of her shoulders' rotation,
elbows almost vertical,
bare arms bewinging her head,
and gathers her hair
within one hand's encompassing.
The other slides a bright
fabric band from her wrist
onto the cylindered mass
with the practiced motion of
some slight-of-hand illusion,
the topological description of which
would require several pages
of elaborate equations.
The hair is pulled into a tight
helmet of russet, streaked
with gold against her head,
the surplus coiled, implicate
with itself, intricate
as an Escher *trompe-l'oeil*,
escaping filaments, glistening
tendrils in hyperbolic curves and spirals,
like cosmic rays caught in a bubble chamber.
Fingers, long and pale and slender,
slither, roving, probing
the labyrinthing strands,
twining like luminous serpents
plaiting, mating in a darkling sea.
And having thus immobilized
her prey, she turns
and consumes it
with a smile.

In Absentia

Moonlight breaks itself
on garden stones,
searching anxiously along
gleaming latitudes
of snail silver,
leading nowhere, everywhere.

Lawn chairs, still
dazed from their dozing,
stare in stupor, amazed
at their abandonment.

Grieving crickets encounter
only the unechoed
emptiness
their love songs
now elicit.

Ardent roses release
prisoned scent,
vain enticement,
dissipated now among
noseless toads.

The long-limbed live oak,
suppliant in all directions,
has no one to lean upon,
and the grass beneath
its boughs, shivers
from the absence
of an accustomed warmth.

The helpless stars,
themselves, blink back
uncomprehending tears,
distraught that your eyes
no longer mirror
their mystery.

Blackberry Eden

Suddenly globuled,
      like black holes gobbling
            their white dwarf flower stars,
wild blackberries,
      appear in profusion,
            catching us unprepared.
Yet, undeterred,
      we catch them, too,
            in bellied T-shirts,
and gorge,
      gashed vermilion
            staining fingers and faces.
Your long hair tangles
      in cat-clawed brangles,
            and you squeal
with only half-feigned fear,
      for here the copperhead
            is known to lair.
So, sweating
      in the danger-heavy air,
            your upper lip
glistening erotically
      in this impossible place,
            we dance
a chary bolero among the thorns,
      emerging with
            their script inscribed
on abdomen and arms,
      carry off their dark treasure
            to feast upon at leisure,
and even dream
      the berries in our beds,
            taunted and entangled
by thorn fronds, each fruit
      an ebon panther's eye,
            eluding and alluring us
                into the labyrinth.

Days later we return with buckets,
but the berries have all shriveled
to dark pinheads in the heat.
Only bare, brown, angry canes remain,
skeletal stalks, still menacing,
yet, already aestivating.
Will it be the same with us?

Why Is the Speed of Light So Slow?
(a quantum physics love poem)

Why is the speed of light so slow?
        Oh, yes, just between us,
                it's sufficiently frisky to see by.
But if I'm on the moon, it takes
        an extra second to hear your voice,
                even if you shout.
If light leaped as swiftly as desire,
        it might ride the inner curve
                of the universe
all the way around in time
        for us to watch our hearts
                catch fire years ago.
If light played post-prestissimo,
        we'd all be geniuses!
                Our synapses
would fairly scintillate with ratiocination.
        Then I might think fast enough
                to say some right thing to you.
But, no, I'm left speechless
        by the laggardness
                of light.
And, yes, light's fleet enough
        to keep our bodies from collapsing
                into tiny singularities
and prevents us from melting
        into each other.
                But would that be so bad?

We cannot ever even really touch.
Our constituent atoms repel
each other with photon streams,
light waves leaping from electrons,
as our bodies proximate,
attempt to bless each other
in this quantum pyrotechnical night.
We each are ancient starlight,
sparkling for but a moment,
sending bright signals through frigid infinities,
and all too often we are absent when
those rays reach where we have been.
Why is the speed of light so slow?

Multiverse

No man is an island? *Au contraire!*
We each are entire universes,
hermetically sealed from one another.
And though we may seem to perceive
the same sensations, ideas, impulses,
we can never know for sure
that what we both call red,
your eyes may really see as green,
or that your taste for Cabernet
is more complex than my tongue can convey.
We can't inhabit another's universe;
we can but sometimes signal each other,
across our infinite divide, with vague pheromones,
with twitches of our exterior topology,
even with crudely modulated auditory wave
functions, wriggling atoms of atmosphere
giggling in our ears, or with these inadequate,
transitory scribbles on this already self-devouring page.
Do your quanta dance to the same constants as mine?
Is entropy the inexorable decay of beauty into chaos
in your universe as in mine?
You are an enigma cocooned in a cosmos
containing a strange attractor.
If only I had a multiverse, inter-dimensional, warp drive
powerful enough to propel me into your universe
—but then Scotty would roar: "Captain,
if I push the engines harder, they're surely gonna blow!"
If only I could somehow asymptote your event-horizon,
feel my space-time distorted by the embrace
of your galaxy's great attractor.
I'm eager to endure your gravities, to spend my life
navigating your unnamed constellations,
exploring your glowing globular clusters,
for gazing deep into your universe's eyes,
I see such enticing, alien stars.

TimemiT

(Note to reader: read each alternate line from right to left as indicated by the arrows. This emphasizes the poem's concept of time reversing itself)

According to Einstein, there's no reason ⤶
.backward run shouldn't time
Perhaps the universe breathes ⤶
exhalations and—in chronologic as time ⤶
that rhythmically reverse ⤶
.events time's of flow the ⤶
Surely time is conserved ⤶
.matter and energy are as just ⤶
So some temporal mirror may reflect ⤶
.itself upon back time ⤶
We would not be aware ⤶
,reversal the of ⤶
mired as we are in ⤶
.ignorance ,flesh ,time ⤶
Backflow would seem only natural: ⤶
,chaos from waking aged the ⤶
growing younger, smaller, ⤶
inside sucked being ⤶
their mother's wombs, ⤶
.disappear to ⤶
Death on either end of time's tether ⤶
.certain as just is ⤶
We are composed of time, ⤶
,sea (endless?) its in ripples ⤶
existing only because time tides ⤶
eternity one toward ⤶
or another. ⤶
perceive could I If ⤶
time's retrograde metachronistically, ⤶
everything hear might I ⤶
you've heard come ⤶
,ears your from singing ⤶

30

see your visions flooding
,eyes your from Technicolor
and feel again your tranquil hands
puzzle the unsolving
of my face,
flowing tears
from your fingertips
,eyes my to untimely
both of us lost
eternal sweet in
timelessnesses.

Red Rover

Their arms unfold, extend with exquisite simultaneity,
one on Mars, another couched on Earth
stretching to cover her cold shoulder.
The mechanical arm deploys a million-dollar drill
to scratch the stony skin of Mars.
She casually shrugs away his hand.

He always wanted to be an astronaut, you know.
But the eyes weren't quite twenty twice.
He pled he'd give an arm to go.
They said no one-armed astronauts allowed.
He became an engineer instead.

Having no life of his own, he designed
lives for beings even more mechanical than he.
Had designs on her, too. Blazed
with data when she smiled.
But when he told her she could have
his heart, she would not have him—heartless.

It requires four minutes at the speed of light
to send a command to the Mars Rover
and an equal interval for its reply.
Time enough for anyone to think
what might be better said
between would-be lovers.
But here on Earth, only micro-second eternities
apart, we often become dataless,
lose contact, wander aimlessly amuck.

They eye the tube. Its popping phosphors
recursed fifty times a second
(if things change fast enough
we think they have not changed at all).
We really know nothing of NOW.
We all live eighty microseconds ago,
the time it takes a nerve impulse to

travel from an eye or finger
to snap a synapse in our prefrontal lobe
and paint a new picture of outer reality.

Why do we find it awesome
that starlight we see may be
centuries old, yet fail to wonder
that we must recreate the world anew
each second,
as it was eighty microseconds ago,
just to take a step, to feel an embrace,
to catch another's eye,
to recognize friend from foe,
to find she's turned away her face.

From carrion comfort, they contemplate
this desolate existence.
The robot goes on exploring Mars,
a foreign body performing its duties,
dutifully seeking evidence of life,
glimmer of meaning, modicum of hope.
Though once, perhaps, something briefly flowed
here, millennia ago,
now there is nothing left
but cold and dust.

Ill Wind

Gloss on Western Wind

Western wind, when will thou blow
      The small rain down can rain?
Christ, if my love were in my arms
      And I in my bed again!
                  Anonymous

Western wind, when will thou blow
to shake the trees from frigid sleep,
to stir to fire my sullen cinders,
to spin my sparks up toward tender,
to flame my soul upon the deep.
Western wind, when will thou blow

the small rain down may rain?
No hands can such small rain hold.
The rain that seeks a root to bless
within the dumb heart's emptiness.
What unkind prophesy foretold
the small rain down may rain?

Christ, if my love were in my arms
the world would dim to just us two.
But neither wind nor I shall lift her hair,
the rain fall only on despair,
for she is gone to you.
Christ, if my love were in my arms,

and I in my bed again!
My bed that was our universe
cannot now contain my sorrow.
What matter if rain or wind tomorrow?
Now there is only bad and worse,
and I in my bed again!

Heart Stone

I kept a cautious stone
against my heart
all those long days
and years,
afraid it would be swallowed
by the world.
But then you came
and rolled the stone away,
infused my heart with
infrangible love,
confuting all
my fears,
and taught my heart
to swallow the world.

Bowen
2007

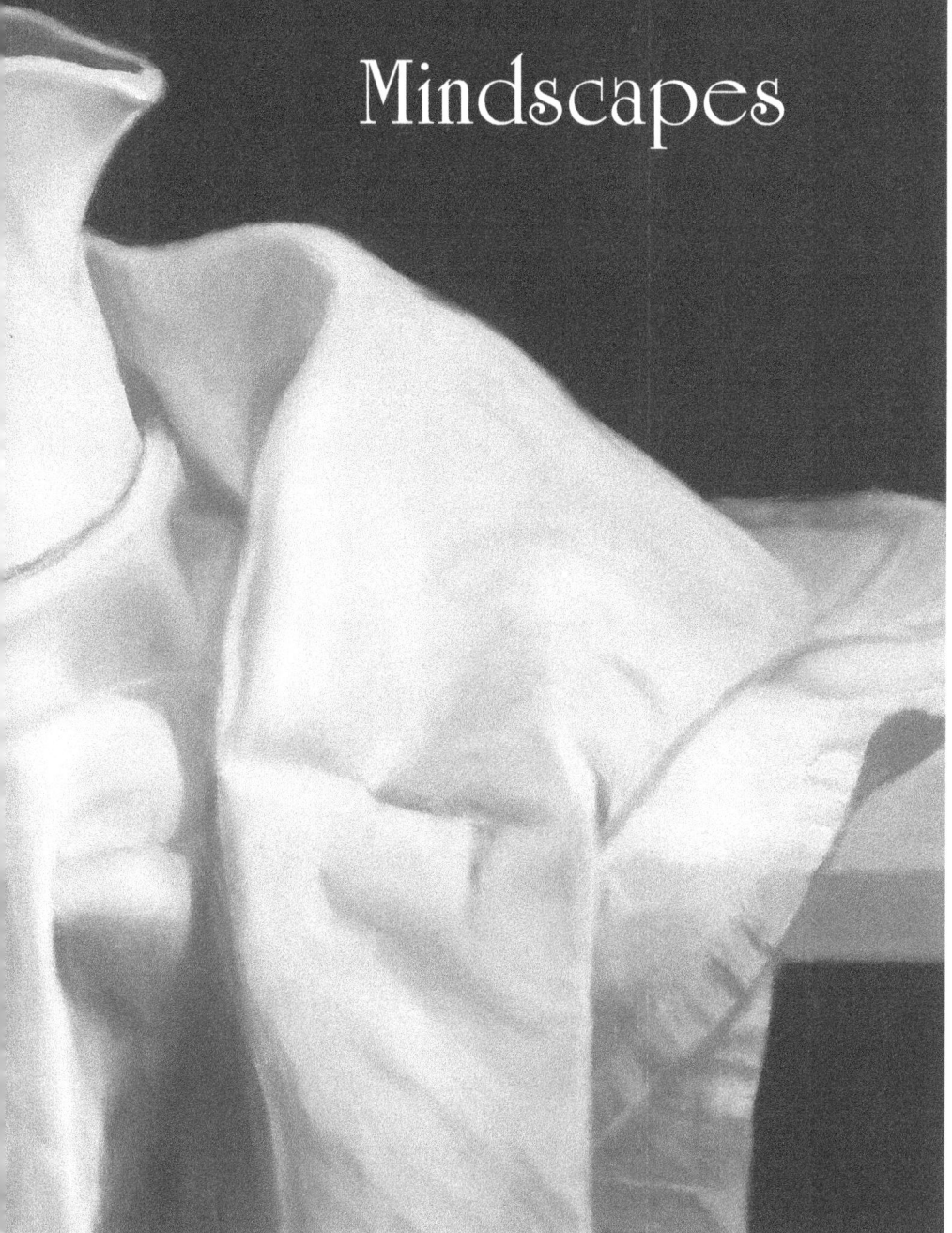

Mindscapes

Memento Vivre (Remember You Must Live)

> For Beauty is nothing
> but the beginning of Terror
> we are still just able to bear.
> Rainer Maria Rilke, *First Duino Eligy*

Have you noticed lately that you're dead?
At least, all that we see of each other is dead:
our hair, our nails, our skin—
all dead.
Even the corneas of our eyes,
clear clothing the inner shine of iris,
are transparently
dead.
And we exude death constantly:
our bodies shed some two thousand dead cells—
every second.
They must be both quick and dead
to make way for ever more dead cells rising as they die—
hallelujah!
We wear death constantly as protection
against a hostile external environment of
palpable harms, eager pathogens,
aggressive putrescences,
poetry critics.
Ironically, it is with the dead surface
of ourselves that we most deny death.
Our inner churning liquid slick and slimy liveness
we find unbearably repulsive to contemplate.
So we deem our dead exteriors
beautiful
and we obsess upon that deadly beauty,
which will devour us.

We diligently design our death masks,
and we split them open
with undead tongues,

grinning like rumba mummies at a minuet,
fearfully frenetic in our efforts to forget
the horror of our aliveness,
the realization that these fragile shells
we so tenuously inhabit
are really trembling tenements of bacteria,
corporate billions of tiny, mindless entities
blindly working with and warring against
themselves, as oblivious to us
as we are to them,
for we quite simply are them —
our constituent bacteria —
patchwork Frankensteins,
squalid colluding colonies of primordial slime,
taking nourishment
from each others' wastes.
Through evolutionary eons,
bacteria have shaped themselves into every
conceivable physical expression, including us.
But we were the first, the only species
to know, to understand, to deny
that we are dead and always dying.

We dwell at the very cusp of chaos,
vacillating among fear, confusion, dogma, delusion,
reluctant to accept our only unique gift,
the emergent magic of self-consciousness.
Whom do we nourish with our fears?
Ignoring the flicker of wings
at the edges of our awareness,
we attend only to the demanding
voices of the unborn.
Our blood, like the sea tide, seeks the moon.
Where is there gravity for the soul?
Why must we die for God's sins?
We have yet to comprehend
the ruthlessness of **Love**.
How, then, shall we remember to Live
except by embracing this terror?

40

Waiting

I wrote this poem as usual,
at the last minute,
waiting for inspiration,
waiting unamused, to be mused, to be
infused with winged fire.
But, of course, I had to hobble instead of fly.
Such is the pattern of my existence:
always waiting for a sign that I should
do some worthy, some wondrous thing,
patient for a more propitious time,
a more appropriate occasion,
yet, somehow, never recognizing it,
until far too late.
Never sure what *diem* to *carpe*.
Always waiting for some *deus ex machina*
to appear and rescue me
from life's wretched ambiguity.
So it seems my moments of possibility
have merely dripped away
rather than riding me high
on a tide of momentousness.
And my story comes down to
an extended series of ellipsis,
a neat, bleak row of ink dots leading
nowhere, and only there to indicate
the absence of what might have happened
if only I hadn't waited for....

(Note to reader: if reading to an audience, rap the lectern several times at the end)

When Neither Truth Nor Beauty Come

When neither truth nor beauty come,
still, life limps on, or leaps beyond our choosing.
Illegitimi non carborundum.

What once inspired, expired within my cranium.
My muse is surely dead, not merely snoozing,
when neither truth nor beauty come.

Then my soul's fire seems a crematorium
and the world's woes well worth losing.
Illegitimi non carborundum.

Doesn't take a truck to crush a chrysanthemum.
The worm that flies by night is not amusing
when neither truth nor beauty come.

I've lived well beyond the millennium,
yet, my heart's not inured to bruising.
Illegitimi non carborundum.

Only fools try truant to life's curriculum,
but if spirit's sparks find flesh refusing
when neither truth nor beauty come:
*illegitimi non carborundum!**

---

*"*Illegitimi non carborundum*" is a mock-Latin aphorism jokingly taken to mean "Don't let the bastards grind you down". It originated during World War II. The phrase was adopted by US Army general "Vinegar" Joe Stillwell as his motto during the war. It was further popularized in the US by President Harry Truman and by 1964 presidential candidate Barry Goldwater.

Suicide Sans Sui

"while living be dead, completely dead,
and do as you please, all will be well." The Buddha

>breathing up a birdless sky
>these sibling stones know one thing
>the blind moon smiles like Mona Lisa
>what cage will confine
>an unquickened heart
>   never mind

>listening for the trickle of timefullness
>sweet music drips from fingers and toes
>the moth with burned-away wings
>dreams still of the flame
>what to do when one can conjure
>only imaginary toads
>   never mind

>shake loose this japing shadow
>no horizon will rim this empty wind
>now when only too much is enough
>fat black apples laugh wormlessly
>what eats the eaters of the dead
>   never mind

>perhaps the earth will end
>not in ice or fire
>but in the desicated husk
>of exhausted desire
>how many zeitgeists can dance
>on a cathode ray
>   never mind

>careless of this feckless mechanism
>hesitant above the chasm
>caught between cold careening stars
>and occult decaying molecules
>entropy works its oxymoronic

43

sardonic grimace over each least
introspective glance
let these sly bones have one last dance
before embracing oblivion
but who pursues the furies
                    never mind

even the unfinished symphony
                    stops

Ghost Guessed

We gossamer ghosts,
       dream-drawn ambient echoes,
trespassing effortlessly
       through our afterlives,
sourceless music ensorceling
       any who listen unintendedly,
blending in the scenery, unseen,
       except sometimes in the quiver
of unquiet air, unthere, until
       caught briefly in a cornered eye, or
breathlessly by those joining us
       impendingly.

You rude husks who hosted us
       in dreary materiality,
extrapolating your desires and fears
       endlessly until the end,
little understand with just your
       meat mentality.
Friend, what we are is unexplainable
       while yet unattainable.
There's far more to know than even
       Hamlet told Horatio.
And in this endless Möbius movement,
       perhaps we, too, are all
merely reincarnate ghosts
       of ghosts.

Angels

Pity the poor angels.
They have been enslaved, exploited,
aggrieved, and abandoned.
When we were prehistoric pantheists,
we knew them as nature spirits,
investing every rock and tree with sacred significance.
Then Jehovah bought them two for a nickel
and hied them to heaven to prepare his palaces.
When some rebelled, he gave them Hell to raise.
The rest became general flunkies.
Late-comer Allah had to lease his
from big J's used angel lot,
and he must have had bad credit or something,
cause J and A have been feuding ever since,
us and the angels caught
in the middle with divided disloyalties.
Then came the Nietzchean news
that God was dead.
And a lot of folks believed it, even though
others say he just got an MBA and changed his name.
Now all the angels have been downsized,
and we see them on almost every street corner:
once proud Seraphim scrabbling for cigarette butts,
pathetic Cherubim passed out drunk in the gutter,
vacantly gazing at the stars.
Still, they get some handouts and they are becoming
adept at dumpster diving (though it's hard on the wings).
Angels stare haggardly at us from battered
cardboard boxes (their degraded connection to trees),
ultimate refugees, begging for a homeland or a handout.
It's sad, but those who can't adapt to change
are doomed to dance on pinheads.
Anyway, let me reassure you that no angels
were harmed in the writing of this poem.

God's Suicide Note

You'll know I'm dead,
not when it begins to rain
broken angels,
but well before then.
Even before you feel the up-rip of soul
that you hadn't known was there,
which, like a gut-hooked fish
suddenly unoceaned, knows, only then,
what water is by its absence.
No, even before that absoluteness,
you may have a sense of *déjà vu perdu*,
a *frisson sans raison*,
not because of the advance
of ordinary evil (that has always been
your God-given right). Rather,
when the Word becomes absurd—
when music makes cacophony
of deliberate monotony —
when religion is loveless legalism—
when the mind is blind to wonder—
when nature is known only unnaturally—
when the rose weeps, but you cannot—
Then, you may suspect the truth, but
it will already be too late.
Still, there will always be time for you
to understand the emptiness
of eternity.

Pictures

We saw the historic picture of the mushroom cloud
blooming in a flash, consuming the city,
lashing out as shock wave, shattering everything,
then its death wind sucking in dust to feed
its sudden emptiness.
And we said, let this picture remind us
that we must learn to love and to trust.
But only fear could feed our emptiness;
so we built ten thousand more bombs.

We saw the picture of the earth from space,
a serene blue marble, a bright brave bubble,
alone in vasting nothingness,
pirouetting thru frigid darkness,
a fragile basket containing all our eggs.
And we said, let this picture remind us
that we must protect the earth, our mother.
But greed and willing ignorance ate us;
so we raped her as our fathers did before.

We saw pictures of our proud towers
struck to rubble in a moment, saw
the smoke of thousands of souls ascending,
mindful crimes from mindless malice,
fruit of a hundred years of plunder.
And we said, let this picture remind us
we all are brothers and can bless each other.
But we pledged ourselves to vengeful gods,
so we doomed another generation of children.

Soon, perhaps, we will need no more pictures.

Global Warming

Glaciers are calving icebergs fast as rats reproduce.
One third of Earth's water is glacial ice.
But not for much longer.
Goodbye Venice; goodbye Houston!
Weather is wilder; hurricanes are havocking.
Gaia is having a hot flash.
But for her it's only momentary;
twenty or thirty thousand years at most.
Of course we probably won't be around by then.
Perhaps some more deserving, wiser, or
less rapacious creature will replace us
in the great chain of being and becoming.
Gaia won't mourn us. She couldn't care less
if we survive, thrive, or disappear.
She has experienced hundreds of major changes
in her biosphere, many lasting millions of years.
She has always managed to restore
the balance of nature, the harmonious
interdependence of all living things.
But regaining her balance this time
will probably mean eliminating seven billion
silly humans who are giving her the itches.
And when we are gone,
we will have the dubious distinction of being
the only species in history to commit suicide.
All other mass extinctions have been caused by
an external factor, such as the demise
of the dinosaurs by meteor impact.
We have fouled our own nest, poisoned ourselves
with our own wastes, and now we've stuck our heads
in the global oven and turned on the gas.
Yet, all the while, we tell ourselves
global warming is just a tree-hugger's exaggeration,
and anyway, technology will save us,
and, besides, we really have no "viable" alternative
to the wasteful, destructive way we live.
So much for Gaia's experiment with intelligence.

She probably won't make that mistake again.
But what's truly sad is that before we make
our ignominious exit, we will have caused the extinction
of so many other beautiful, innocent species.
And it's not as if we weren't warned.
Whales have been singing their lamentations
across the oceans and beaching themselves
in symbolic gesture for generations.
Butterflies, birds, and gentle frogs,
in their weakened numbers, reproach us.
Pray that we will not be called to account
for our crimes against the earth,
for we were given paradise
and we have made it a slag heap and worse.
But, hey, we took far more
than thirty pieces of silver in the process.

Lizard Lecture

Tricking the bricks into believing
  she is one of them,
a speckled gecko and I perform
  our Sunday morning rituals on the back patio,
I, slurping coffee while perusing the news
  for the most recent societal excrescences;
she, more practically engaged in providing
  sticky-tongued obituaries for unwary insects.
She seems so omnipotent on her wall,
  proud, puny monarch of those bare, few square yards.
I warn her to keep an eye cocked
  for the backyard cat and the brash bluejay.
But, she ignores my wise counsel, boldly pursuing
  her reptilian entrepreneurialism.
I think she'll not last long, basking on the bricks,
  drowsy after breakfast.
If she could only comprehend me across these
  barely intersecting boundaries of our divergent realities.
Ah, well, I must return to life's earnest concerns. Yet,
  she seems intent now on catching my eye,
and her lipless little mouth is open
  as if she's about to speak.

Not About Butterflies

They warn you in workshops
not to write poems about butterflies.
It marks you as a sentimentalist
and a dilettante.
Yet, butterflies are so beautiful
it's always a temptation
to poetize them.

Butterflies perceive many more colors
than do we, thus to appreciate
the beauty of flowers and of each other.
Butterflies even have eyes
on their genitals so as to admire
the magnificence of their coupling.

Butterflies make the earth orgasmic
with flowers. They can see
ultraviolet fluorescences of nectar
in the vaginal deepnesses of flowers,
taste with filamented feet
the flowers' sweet clinging semen dust,
and so become literal love notes
from one flower to another.

Butterflies calligraphify the wind
with evanescent messages
of possibly ultimate meaning writ
in bright balletic movements understood
only by themselves and God.

Butterflies are so beautiful
sometimes we don't even kill them,
despite their lack of economic value.
Ah, such blatant sentimentality!
That's why this poem
is not about butterflies.

Wasps

It happens every summer.
The wily red wasps sneak in when
our eyes are on the flowers,
and soon spit out a *papier-mâché*
mushroom home hanging
under the guttered eaves.
By the time we become aware,
the wasps are agossip
in their paper apartments,
smirking of their *fait acompli*
and popping out new broods daily.
We tolerate each other except
when they construct too close
to the back door, and become
irritable about our frequent
in's and out's. Finally,
I have to smack them with my
wasp whopper, sending their nest
plummeting into the backyard grass,
quickly to be abandoned
to ravening fire ants.
I'm always sorry to dispossess them.
I hope our buzzing nest of humanity
hasn't been built too close
to someone's cosmic back door.

Meditation on Basho's Frog

An old pond: a frog jumps in—
the sound of water.   Basho

His golden eyes emerge again,

bulging up the liquid skin,

yet silent and rippleless

amid a maze of watercress.

Eyes which must survey

for both predator and prey

must encompass many radii

of earth, of water, and of sky.

Optics thus designed must choose

what to see and what to lose.

Only movement is frog-known;

all else is shadow, light, water, stone.

Our frog, with motion-actuated eyes,

would starve amid a static feast of flies.

Are we, like frogs, some-wise deficient,

ignoring what could be nourishment?

To what, then, are we blind

who follow but the movement of the mind?

Metamorphosis

And does the ravening caterpillar,

    methodically devouring

    the leaf beneath her,

    when the first deep tremble

    of nascent wing muscle,

    unrecognized, rumbles

    through the green length of her,

    pausing her marauding mandibles

    for the first time,

    causing her to arch her

    bristled cylinder rampantly

    above the leaf's horizon

    and to look with insect awe

    upon the immensity of the world

    for but a few swaying,

    vertiginous seconds

    before she shudders

    with the pupal imperative

    to weave her cocoon,

        believe it will be her coffin?

The Journey

Based on the painting, Ozark Memory, by Johnny Bowen

Trails were worn thru wilderness
by migrating beasts and man,
since time immemorial.
Man evolved to wander,
following herds as hunter-gathers
for myriad millennia. So wander-lust
is the very marrow of our bones,
the plural branching pathways of our brains.
We still journey from unknown to unknown,
wandering aimlessly or aimed, mind-maimed,
questing a path from our dark forest
into that golden, sunlit country
of fulfilled desire. Forgetting
that utopia means nowhere.
Who are we who obsessively search,
enduring hardships and humiliations,
for we really know not what?
Where are the beauty and wonder
we have lost in treading only
the well-trampled road?
We instinctively seek
an ever elusive something, some
where that is not here,
a perfect end of
an imperfect journey,
only to find, in the end,
just the journey itself.

Moondrunk Lunar Eclipse

nothing more naked than moonlight
she dances Salome's solemn bacchanal
upon the wine-dark night while
we and the stars drown moondrunk
nothing more drunk than moondrowned
while we prattle on of stock picks   politics   jazz licks
until brightness fails as she unveils
and blushes with shadowed innocence
nothing more innocent than moonblush
yet as she unmirrors the sun
and echos earth's lesser lumination
could love thus reflect if only in eclipse
nothing more reflective than moonlove
so we see her shed her last
bright sliver shivering mindless
perhaps not only with the cold
nothing more shiverous than moonmind
then slowly she hurtles
homeless as a god-thrown stone
lost on her always falling circle
nothing more homeless than moonlost
and we stagger blindly back inside
only to find her stranded in the television
wonder-wounded
nothing more

The Why of White

Based on the painting, The Why of White, by Johnny Bowen

What is the why of white?
There are so many ways of seeing.
Everything is made of light.

Where there is no day or night,
no floor or wall or ceiling.
What is the why of white?

There is a deepness more than bright,
as if some essence freeing.
Everything is made of light.

What mystery do some things excite?
Might objects' souls elicit this awed feeling?
What is the why of white?

Only truest art can get it right,
this absolute of saying.
Everything is made of light.

Some things require an unseen sight.
They radiate the weight of being.
What is the why of white.
Everything is made of light!

The Heart Has Its Reasons

Le coeur a ses raisons que la raison ne connaît point.
Pascal, *Pensées*

The heart has its reasons that the reason knows not of.
The heart in its season flows both blood and tears.
We are made to suffer that we may learn to love.

Where is the hidden hand that fits this worn, old glove,
the hand that could dispel unreasoned fears?
The heart has its reasons that the reason knows not of.

Crushed between the push of time and callous shove
of unkind circumstance, suffocating through the years:
we are made to suffer that we may learn to love.

Within the tangled ganglia unwitting soul is wove.
Where is soul's reason in that forest if no one hears?
The heart has its reasons that the reason knows not of.

Weep, then, or rage at the silence from above.
What moves in mystery may suffer other cares.
We are made to suffer that we may learn to love.

We are but the sum of all our terrors until we heart the dove.
Though we suffer for a reason, it's not what it appears.
The heart has its reasons that the reason knows not of.
We are made to suffer that we may learn to love.

Soulscapes

Bowen

Abortion

Forgive me,
for I know what I have done.
I cannot deny that you were
and would have been.
I can only pray that you, greedy
for life, felt no pain.
Were you aware and did you
struggle in panic when
the ravening suction
sought you, brought your
tight little universe once more
to the chaos
from which it had so
miraculously emerged?
We had become two opposed
imperatives in one flesh.
Only I had the power to chose; yet
I really had no choice.
For to let you live could only
desolate both our lives.
Why must our most important choices
always lie among evils?
Goodby, child who could not be.
The world is not yet
good enough for you,
nor for me.
I must seek to make it so.

What He Died Of

It was not the broken bones
that killed him.
His young body quickly mended them.
He was not killed by the cuts and burns
that pictographed his skin
with scenes of horror.
The hunger and isolation of being locked
for days in the dark closet
did not kill him.
That was almost a welcome respite.
Nor did he die of the beatings
from the drunks and addicts that
populated his short life.
It was not even his shoe strings,
really, that killed him
when he hung himself
in his cell in juvenile detention.
No, it was not the violence
that killed him.
He couldn't have told you
what it was.
He never knew what
lack it was he died of,
long before.

A Hunger for Genius

I have never been hungry for more than an hour.
So please excuse the ineptitude, the presumption
of this poem, the want of power. I am an unequal surrogate
for one who could tell of hunger from direct experience.
But she is absent, her poems unwritten, and we are the poorer.
She would have been the finest poet of her generation.
Instead she knew not just hunger but starvation.
Her body, mind, and spirit shriveled ere they could bloom.
She died not in a house or hospital room but outside in heat
and dust because, none but the flies knew who she was.
She was but a tiny girl of nine with bloated belly
and arms and legs as thin as twine.
Her mind had homed a genius fire to learn, to create,
to imagine the sweetness of a thousand possibilities.
She will not be honored now, nor will anyone know or care.
Her mother's fingers tangled tender in her hair,
she died of hunger, her mother of despair.
She was Kurdish, Tutsi, Afganistani, Brazilian,
Armenian, Azerbijani, Chinese, Iraqi, Palestinian,
and, yes, she was American.
At the end she did not think of food; the pain was too intense.
Yet, there was no blood. Her body devoured itself
in self-cannibalism, a slow and painful feast.
The starving body is an implacable, uncomprehending beast.
How many Mozarts, Picassos, Curries, Einsteins,
Dickinsons have we lost to hunger?
How many unknown geniuses has the earth sucked under?
Excuse the ineptitude of this poem.
It is a partial penance, though without consolation,
for I have seen the eyes of hunger and of desperation
and done nothing.

Personal Permutations

Sometimes it's hard to be kind
when even the stink of death
goes unnoticed when
you habit with corpses.

Sometimes it's kind to be hard.
Must we be murdered into life,
have every moment conspire
to remind us of our nakedness?

Sometimes, to be is kind of hard.
We somnolent shadows
pass through each other,
intersecting, interpenetrating
effortlessly, fecklessly, obliviously.

Some kind of hard times it's to be
when we say with *schaden-freude,*
"There but for the grace of God go I."
So, self-cocooned, we cannot feel
the same heart beating in everyone.

Some kind time to be of, it's hard.
Yet, love, too, can be harder than diamond.
Perhaps we can't return to Eden.
But maybe life will blink
if we can look it steadfast, loving, in the eye.

Xmas Epiphany

Downtown Houston, mid-December,
chill enough to spill a drizzle,
extravagant with gigawatts of neon,
argon, mercury vapor,
sodium, sulfur, chlorine phosphor,
pointillistic lumination,
miles of lights limn arrogant towers,
smearing spectral brightness on the night.

From far suburban sanctuaries
these must seem God's Christmas tree,
surely visible from space.
But down on near-deserted streets:
a lightmare, a crazy rain
of color-cursed photons
makes sickly shadows in a dozen directions.
The vacant, weird-lit misty plaza,
like an opening scene from some ghost opera.

Why was I startled, then, by your sudden
apparition as I emerged my cab?
You were thin and brown
as a lost sparrow's feather,
holding tightly to your trembling breast
the tiniest baby I had ever seen,
emaciated Madonna.
I was afraid you wanted to give me the child.
"Justa dolla mista; milk fo tha chile."
I could barely hear your whisper.

Those eerie lights reflected from your dark
eyes with a mesmeric intensity, not of anger or
demand but with an implacable dignity of need.
And I, cashless in my expensive suit, ashamed,
rebuffed you silently and slithered into the hotel.

Years later your beautiful, terrible eyes
still reproach me. Was it just
those mist-mad Christmas lights?

A Grocery Epiphany

Can you believe it! A dozen coconut macaroons for $3.99!
That's a week's wages for people in Cameroon.
(Would a Cameroon eat a macaroon with a finger or a spoon?)
But I do love a macaroon in the afternoon with tea.
So into my grocery basket they go.
And the price of seedless grapes…
(were these seeds extracted by movie stars or corporate CEO's?)
You've got to check them, too, because they try to hide
the squished ones in the middle of the bag. However,
there's nothing as refreshing as frozen grapes in summer heat,
so they, too, are remanded to my basket.

Of course they don't have the canned tuna my cat prefers,
so I settle for the whitefish and hope Fluff doesn't get finicky.
Then the kid in the basket ahead cranks up the volume
on his "I want it Momma" whine, while Mom
blocks the aisle, blabbering obliviously on her cell phone.
While she's turned the other way, I hand the whiner
a package of cookies in easily ripped cellophane,
then make a quick exit to the next aisle,
just in time to hear Mom's hideous shriek of maternal betrayal.
A cookie rolls around the corner toward me accusingly,
but now I am cruising toward the checkout counter
with a sneer of victory.

.

Once in line, of course, I remember I need cantaloupes, too.
But now I'm boxed in by an ancient doddering couple
who have moved their basket in behind me.
They have only a few items so I'm considering
how to tactfully insist they move
to the twelve-items-or-less counter,
when the check-out clerk squawks "Next!".

She's a gum-clacking, vacuum-eyed automaton,
and I barely contain a snarl as I unload
my over-priced merchandise onto the conveyor
where it is swept along to be beeped at by
the red-eyed snake head she fondles
like a priestess of some ancient pagan blood cult.

"Oh, you have a kitty cat!" exclaims the sack girl
with such joyous *élan*, I notice her for the first time.
She's a neat, plain girl with mild Down's Syndrome.
Her eyes gaze into mine with such deep directness
I cannot look away.
She is like a friendly cat, herself, smiling and purring
and looking me steadily in the eye,
while her hands deftly identify each item
and place it gently in the gaping plastic bag.
"I have a kitty, too," she says. "But my kitty likes
tuna better than this," (speaking *sotto voce*, to me alone).
"My kitty's name is Pumpkin, because she is yellow,
and she likes tuna best," she says.

I realize, then, I have inhaled to reply but cannot,
because her face is suffused with pure radiance,
like sun dazzle from fresh snow.
Her eyes are deep and clear and sparkling.
And though I don't take my eyes from her's,
I somehow know that the other faces around me
are, like flowers, blooming with unearned blessedness.
She touches my trembling hand as she puts the bag in mine
and says "Tell your kitty 'Hi' from Pumpkin."
I manage to gasp "Yes, I will, thank you."
Then, my knees desperate to genuflect, I whisper
"Please, forgive me."
She smiles mysteriously and says,
"Buy the tuna next time."

Ioudenitch Plays Adés' *Darkness Visible*

(with the Fort Worth Symphony, October 9, 2001)

One month beyond

the grim glissandos

of collapsing concrete towers

and sforzando of soul-laden

dust ascending,

the piano probes

a still weeping wound,

flows groaning, keening, insizing

into the angry flesh of it,

incanting an all-devouring darkness,

burning an incendiary absence

in the deep sounding of us, till

coagulating tone clusters

sparkle on the dark,

draw it claustro close

so the music becomes

a mirror for lost light,

and we perceive the secret:

that ultimate darkness

collapses

in its all-gathering gravity

to release

a universe of blessed light.

El Niño

(In memory of Betsy K. who loved nature and the arts)

The autumn rains are premature.
It is the year of *El Niño*,
to be colder and wetter than usual, they say.
The oaks must have known; they tried
to fill the pool with acorns and hurled
them at the house like churlish children.
The chameleons have all gone brown
and wedged themselves in crevices.
The wasps and bees, too, have surrendered,
become lethargic, can't find their way home.
Only the butterflies are still hopeful, hovering
fitfully over pale, ravaged flowers, sucking out
the last of their color and moving on, making
the North wind a flowing mosaic.
Why is everything dancing?
Purple beaded beauty bushes,
snake vines, slender loblollies,
bend and wobble in the wind;
pine Pavlovas entice stolid chestnut Nijinskys.
Stravinsky should have written
his fierce *Sacré* for autumn.
But, perhaps the ancients knew they could not
propitiate winter; there is no mystery in it.
A scrim of rain descends between
the screaming moon and me.
Surging at the windows, the rain rhythms
have the same hissing dissonance
as this Bartok quartet, written in hospital,
a defiant, bitter elegy to himself.
Two wet oak leaves scrabble at the window,
veined like wasted hands, blind hands,
searching for an absent face.
They told me yesterday you were lucid
to the last, telling the hapless minister
about a book you thought he might enjoy.

Great Blue

The sticker on the nearly bumped bumper ahead says
      "Time is God's way of keeping everything
      from happening at once."
      But it seems to me that events clump up
      in our lives like punctuated equilibrium
      in evolution theory. And when the sacred
      pierces the envelope of our mundane reality,
      it occurs as surreal intensity of the ordinary.
Watching the mystery of water lilies becoming
      luminous beneath emphysemic clouds,
      a Great Blue Heron blinks into existence,
      enormous on the border stones of our garden pond.
      His beak seems an angel's sword, his gaunt, grim,
      gray-blue feathers rough as a beggar's blanket.
      Haughty as a samurai, his eye pierces me
      with the same power his beak can strike a fish.
      He contemplates the worried water, then,
      disdainfully, skies with a single heave of wing.
Somnambulating along the hospital sidewalk, I wonder if,
      just before the giant eye is razor-sliced
      in *La Chien d'Andalou*, it saw the truth
      of everything with the amazing clarity of finality.
      I think, too, of how trillions of neutrinos
      are streaming through us every second,
      utterly unnoticed, like receiverless radio waves
      we have not yet learned to listen for, and, perhaps
      carry messages of immense import of which
      we will never be aware.

A seeming scrap of dirty paper resolves itself into a long-dead
    toad, rendered flat as a steamrollered cartoon character.
    A wimpled nun intersects my path leading a file of same-
    skirted little school girls, one of whom smiles slyly
    at me and levitates in a perfect ballet *jetté*.
My father lies, absent-eyed, within his death-womb,
    sprouting plastic umbilicals from every body part
    except his navel. Bones seem desperate to burst
    the shrinking membrane of his skin, all the leaking
    energy of his weakening exerted toward escape.
Mom pulls off the sheet to massage his legs,
    once athlete's legs, now thin as the heron's.
    I start toward the hallway to give them privacy,
    but his finger beckons, his eye fierce with effort,
    his gaze focused through me, beyond me,
    beyond beyond.
Having lost his swallow reflex, he can only
    whisper, which is a blessing,
    his mind having been unclear for several days.
    (He insisted the doctor is a Communist
    serial killer and we should call the FBI.
    I did not try to explain to him that the doctor
    is a confirmed Capitalist who will try
    to keep him alive as long as the insurance holds out).
I put my ear to his hard lips and he whispers, hoarsely:
    "It's so easy to fly when you remove the load."
    Perhaps he was simply referring in some hallucinatory
    way to his career as an aircraft engineer, but—-
    that night my father's scarred soul skied
    with a single heave of heart.

Watching Water Lilies In Rain

Their green hearts inhabit
      the thin infinity between
the pressing of water and sky,
      blessing both, then curling
rainward to become holy chalices.

Their green hearts seem hammered
      tympani in rain's rhythm,
echo and interrupt expanding circles,
      halo hellos
dropped from a cloud's cold mile.

Their green hearts haven a spiked
      purple crown that opens
to lick up lightning where
      there is no sun,
resurrected radiance in ecru rainlight.

My green heart hoards
      this image, a gladsome duty,
sends it soulward, as to a pungent
      thrusting flower, bursting
with the mystery of God's greed for beauty.

Flying on Love

I heard a fly buzz—when I died—
                    Emily Dickinson

I heard a fly buzz when I died
and watched it break
its wings against a lamp
illumined brighter than
the open window's waiting radiance.
What did they make of my last
ironic laugh,
to realize only then
we all are flies
buzzing bewildered
on the very air of love
and never know it's there.

Insoulation

We husk the holy.
We enchrysalise the soul
as it secretes us, seals
itself within, and turns
worm to wing with
our sighs, sins, mercies,
imaginings, prosaic
signals of soul's
enfolding.
So, when our capsule
is sundered
and abandoned on the stem,
wings of latent love
may warm and then
take flight.

A Threnody in Winter

*Walking in the woods after visiting the
Houston Holocaust Museum*

The gaunt moon makes its cold nest in the wind—
A grumpy toad hunkers in a lost summer shoe—
Late daisies limp into winter on toothless unicycles—
Sandhills bow the sky, croaking southlessly—
A sweet gum's yellow star presses to my chest,
then desperately rejoins the leaf storm—
A few new mushrooms struggle bravely up
through decayed manure like naked children—
Skeletal trees, ensnarled by thorn vines,
frighten even the sparrows—
An abandoned burn pile, still smoldering,
exhales smoke flows like writhing shadows—
Pine cone cantatas whisper *"Dies Irae,"*
song of death on the Day of Wrath,
as they scatter thousands of tiny
dead angels' wings—
Now the woods, the wind, the birds are silent—
Soon it will rain,
the rain of forgetting—
Nor will the wind remember—
But the earth—
The earth will always know the truth.

About the Author

MICHAEL BALDWIN is a native of Fort Worth, Texas, where he graduated Salutatorian from Diamond Hill Jarvis High School. He holds a B.A. in Political Science from North Texas State University, and Masters degrees in Public Administration (TCU) and in Library Science (UNT). His career has primarily been that of a public library administrator, but he has also been a Field Operations Supervisor for the 2000 U.S. Census, and a teacher of American Government. He is currently director of the Benbrook Public Library and is CEO of the web business Libraries For Democracy.

Mr. Baldwin's poems stem mostly from an early and enduring love of nature and his exploration of it through science, particularly astronomy. As a youth he constructed a Newtonian telescope and followed the progress of the space program closely. A potential career as an astronaut was cut short when he wrote NASA that he would give his left arm to go into space but was informed that astronauts require both arms. He maintained a biology and chemistry lab in his bedroom closet until the day of the exploding ant farm.

In addition to not having been an astronaut, Mr. Baldwin is also an ex-would-be tennis pro (poetry is much more lucrative), and a jazz clarinetist manqué (the Dregs of Dixieland). He is currently attempting not to be an ex-poet.Baldwin's poetry has been not widely enough published in such journals as *Commonweal, Louisiana Literature, New Texas*, and *Touchstone*. An issue of *Illya's Honey* containing his poems was nominated for the Pushcart Prize. He won the Violet Newton Poetry Prize 2000, and his poems were featured on the national radio show *The Romantic Hours*. He was a juried poet of the Houston Poetry Festival and has presented poetry workshops at the Langdon Literary Arts Festival. Mike is a long-time member of the Poetry Society of Texas and is a member of Texas' oldest poetry organization, The Fort Worth Poetry Society. He founded the ongoing program series 2nd Tuesday Poetry at the Benbrook Public Library. Baldwin has self-published 6 poetry chapbooks, and his *Slam Poetry Manual* was published by the American Library Association.

About the Artist

Panoramic vistas of ancient Ozark mountains lit by the last rays of the setting sun. Hills and valleys covered in the brilliant hues of autumn. Crystal waters flowing through time-eroded landscapes older than Man. These scenes of the natural world are the inspiration for the realistic and intricate oil paintings of local artist **JOHNNY BOWEN**.

His paintings reflect his own sense of wonder and awe of nature, and his techniques follow in the footsteps of the great American landscape artists of the nineteenth century. Johnny's oil painting methods range from highly detailed, brushmark-free landscapes to more impressionistic palette knife paintings. His subject matter has grown to include still lifes. His paintings have been shown in the Arts Center of the Ozarks annual Fall Show for several years, and in 2006 his small landscape "Autumn in the Ozarks" bid for the highest amount in the ACO 5x5 benefit auction.

"I was inspired to begin painting in 1996 after seeing an exhibit of William McNamara watercolor paintings at the Walton Arts Center. I was astounded by his ability to realistically depict the natural beauty of places I had seen in Newton County, such as the Buffalo River."

Initially self-taught, Johnny soon made contact with respected Texas artist Dalhart Windberg, and has been a student of his for the last ten years. "Dal is a true artistic genius. His style of realistic painting is what I wanted to learn, and he has put me light years ahead of where I would have been trying to learn to paint on my own." Johnny's representational realism is influenced by Windberg, as well as by the nineteenth century artists of the Hudson River School.

Johnny grew up in Texas, and met his wife Peggy when they were students at the University of Texas. Soon after marriage and graduation, they moved to Arkansas and have lived in Northwest Arkansas for nearly thirty years. "After traveling around the country, we decided that Northwest Arkansas was as pretty a place as we had seen, and we moved here as soon as we could," Johnny recalls. They have two children who both attended West Fork schools and obtained degrees from Arkansas universities.

In 2006, Johnny left his job as a consulting engineer in Fayetteville to become a professional artist. "My painting heroes include Durand, Church, Moran, and Bierstadt, and I aspire to create the same feeling of the sublime wonder of the natural world as did these great artists." His hobbies include photography, gardening, and astronomy, all of which reflect his appreciation and wonder of the world and the universe in which we live.

www.ingramcontent.com/pod-product-compliance
Lightning Source LLC
Chambersburg PA
CBHW060036050426
42448CB00012B/3032